The Essential Don Coles

The Essential
Don Coles

selected by Robyn Sarah

The Porcupine's Quill

Library and Archives Canada Cataloguing in Publication

Coles, Don
    The essential Don Coles / selected by Robyn Sarah. – 1st ed.

(Essential poets ; 3.)
Poems.
Includes bibliographical references.
ISBN 978-0-88984-312-7

    I. Sarah, Robyn, 1949 – II. Title.
III. Series: Essential poets (Erin, Ont.) ; 3.

PS8555.O439E88 2009   C811'.54   C2008-906936-6

1   2   3   ·   11   10   09

Published by The Porcupine's Quill, 68 Main Street, PO Box 160,
Erin, Ontario NOB 1TO. http://porcupinesquill.ca

Permission from Véhicule Press is gratefully acknowledged for the poems
from Don Coles' *How We All Swiftly: The First Six Books* that appear in this
volume.

Represented in Canada by the Literary Press Group.
Trade orders are available from University of Toronto Press.

We acknowledge the support of the Ontario Arts Council and the Canada
Council for the Arts for our publishing program. The financial support of the
Government of Canada through the Book Publishing Industry Development
Program is also gratefully acknowledged. Thanks, also, to the Government
of Ontario through the Ontario Media Development Corporation's Ontario
Book Initiative.

ONTARIO ARTS COUNCIL
CONSEIL DES ARTS DE L'ONTARIO

Canada Council   Conseil des Arts
for the Arts   du Canada

Table of Contents

7   Foreword

Sometimes All Over (1975)

11   Photograph in a Stockholm Newspaper for March 13, 1910
12   Divorced Child
13   How We All Swiftly
14   Death of Women

Anniversaries (1979)

15   Sampling from a Dialogue
16   William, etc.
17   Codger
18   Not Just Words but World
19   Gull Lake, Alta.

The Prinzhorn Collection (1982)

20   The Prinzhorn Collection
28   Mishenka (in two versions)
30   Major Hoople
32   Abandoned Lover
32   Abrupt Daylight Sadness
33   Landslides (six excerpts)

Landslides (1986)

38   Walking in the Snowy Night
40   Somewhere Far from This Comfort

Forests of the Medieval World (1993)

42   My Son at the Seashore, Age Two
43   Someone has stayed in Stockholm

45   Forests of the Medieval World
48   My Death as the Wren Library
50   Self-Portrait at 3:15 a.m.
51   Untitled

Kurgan (2000)

52   Kingdom
53   Marie Kemp
54   Flowers in an Odd Time
55   Reading a Biography of Samuel Beckett
56   Nurseryschoolers
57   On a Caspar David Friedrich Painting
        Entitled 'Two Men Observing the Moon'
58   Botanical Gardens

61   About Don Coles

63   A Bibliography

Foreword

The young Don Coles was a sojourner, extending a period of
graduate study at Cambridge into a dozen-odd 'wander-years' in
central Europe and Scandinavia. He returned to Canada in 1965, in
his mid-thirties, and only then began writing poems; his first book
did not appear until 1975, and it was not until the appearance of his
seventh, *Forests of the Medieval World*, in 1993, that his poetry began
to receive the notice it deserved. Coles' European interests and
influences served initially to sideline him as a Canadian poet: his early
books appeared at a time when Canada was bent on forging a literary
culture it could call its own. Declining to follow fashion, he continued
to write poems inspired as often by cultural artefacts and the
pleasures of reading as by the personal: a painting, a line from a
literary biography, a scene from a novel could provide the spark. He
eschewed flashiness of any sort, rejected innovation for its own sake,
and applied a highly concentrated craft to the serious contemplation
of what it is to be human. This won him the deep regard of discerning
readers, but not the acclaim lavished on some of his contemporaries.

In selecting for this volume, I thought it best to excerpt as little as
possible and only where excerpts are effective as self-contained poems.
Not represented here are Coles' two book-length sequences, *K in Love*
(a series of verse love letters inspired by the letters of Kafka) and *Little
Bird* (an extended letter-in-verse to his late father). I have tried
nevertheless to show something of Coles' range – the different kinds
of things he does in his poems, and the different modalities in which
he addresses his overarching subject: time's passage.

Any artist must love what fuels his art, but Coles' love for his
subject is also his war with it: in one poem, he refers to time as a
'catastrophe'; in another, as 'Time, the enemy'. In his poetry one feels
the tug of the past on the present, the ever-present tug of the future;
pathos of hindsight, pathos of aging, but also the consolation of
memory. And one feels the *vertigo* of time – notably, in the haunting
'Somewhere Far from This Comfort'.

Of particular interest to Coles are the arrested moments that
survive in photographs, letters, journals: what they tell us, what they
withhold, the signals they relay across years. A number of his poems
begin in contemplation of a photograph – usually from his own

family album, but the example I have chosen ('Photograph in a Stockholm Newspaper for March 13, 1910') describes a family of strangers, nameless and likely long dead, about whom nothing can be known 'except that once they were there'. Enigmatic, these people are 'safe now from even their own complexities' and they seem to the poet 'miraculous'. Surviving in this single, slightly blurred formal portrait, they present the illusion of having escaped life's rough and tumble – what Coles elsewhere calls 'this old, hard business of meddling with time'.

Against such complexities, Coles holds an ideal of the untouched, which we see in the pre-conscious waking state described in 'Untitled' ('I had not sustained any damage at all yet. Whatever was special in me had not been dulled by use or exposure …') – as in the *tabula rasa* of the hockey rink, in 'Kingdom', after the Zamboni has finished its rounds. Given that life must always decline from such perfect states, the tension in his poetry is that of opposites to which he is differently attracted: wandering and restlessness with their associated risks, vs. stasis and patience with their promise of safety, reliability, serenity. Coles can change sides within a single poem: in 'Botanical Gardens', musing on the rooted constancy of trees, he experiences 'sudden remorse' at 'not having lived patiently enough', but soon decides this line of thought is pointless, admitting, 'I never wanted / to stay long anywhere, really.' Still, he is acutely conscious of might-have-beens. Roads not travelled, words not spoken, lives cut short or otherwise unrealized are invoked in 'Someone has stayed in Stockholm', 'Marie Kemp', 'William, etc.', 'Not Just Words but World'.

A secondary theme for Coles is the plight of the overlooked, the helpless, those who cannot speak for themselves. 'Landslides' is a series of compassionate, mostly one-way conversations with his mother in a geriatric care centre. 'Mishenka' considers the case of Leo Tolstoy's illegitimate half-brother, who grew up illiterate and died a pauper. In 'The Prinzhorn Collection' – a poem that has been compared to Browning's 'My Last Duchess' – a fictional curator writes a letter describing his museum's current exhibition: drawings and writings by inmates of a nineteenth-century German insane asylum, reportedly salvaged by a doctor named Prinzhorn from the files of a predecessor. (The Prinzhorn Collection is real, though Coles has simplified its provenance here.) Through the voice of this conflicted but not unfeeling curator, Coles describes actual drawings from the collection, and quotes passages from heart-rending letters that were never mailed – 'derelict hundred-year-old signals (airless cries, unlit gestures)' that, in coming to light and being presented now as art, stand as both chilling indictment and exigent human truth.

Much has been written of Coles' signature poetic voice – civilized yet informal, poised between colloquial and literary. His poems seem thought-aloud, unfolding spontaneously, with hesitations, backtrackings, and parenthetical digressions that enact a conversational intimacy while guarding a personal privacy. Their casualness is artful: the poems are much more worked than they appear. (One American poet-critic wrote me, 'Reading Coles has been interesting, in that lines that I thought were insufficiently charged the first time through, seem tighter and more satisfying each time I go back to them.') Rhyme, present in some of the earlier poems, is so unobtrusive that an inattentive reader could miss it altogether: see 'Mishenka (I)', 'William, etc.', and 'Sampling from a Dialogue' (the latter actually a disguised Petrarchan sonnet in which, ingeniously, formal moves of the poem slyly echo emotional moves of the couple depicted). Coles is also capable of seamless and inspired vocal shifts: in 'Codger', note how we start out looking at the old man from the outside, but gradually are drawn into his world, until we find ourselves overhearing his very thoughts.

For all that, there's a curious elasticity to Coles' exactness. His fondness for reworking poems is well known: some exist in as many as five or six published versions. While successive revisions show inarguable improvements, each version has its own virtues and its own integrity of logic and effect. The poem remains recognizably itself, but a line-by-line comparison with the previous version will reveal subtle but significant variation throughout (including, often, all new line breaks). One cannot easily splice versions in the interest of saving preferred bits from each; they resist combination. What will future anthologists and editors make of this? For Coles, the latest version of a poem is the definitive one; but the existence of multiple versions will, I suspect, ultimately be recognized as part of the richness of his art.

– ROBYN SARAH

9

Warmest of thanks to Robyn Sarah, who thought this book up and actually edited it, a rare act these days.

Photograph in a Stockholm Newspaper
for March 13, 1910

Here is a family so little famous their names
are not recorded. They stand, indistinct
as though they know it's right, in this slum
courtyard in weak sunlight. The darksuited
father's hand rests on his small son's shoulder,
mother and daughter are on either side of
the open door. It is a Sunday or we may be sure
they would not be together like this, motionless
for the photographer's early art.

To be moved by these people must seem sentimental.
We're here years too late to hope their paused
faces will unpack into features we can side with or
against, or expect these bodies will release themselves
into those next shapes on which we'll base a plot.

But that's it: not here they are, but there they
were. Safe now from even their own complexities –
what luck not to be asked their names! – and proof
against our most intricate pursuit, they stand in
a blur that seems no error of focus but an inspired
rendering of how they chose to last, admitting
nothing except that once they were there. That hand
rested on that shoulder. The four of them stood
there. The door was left open. There was
a little sunlight.

We shall never learn more. They seem miraculous.
They persuade me all may be well.

Divorced Child

away from those bad voices now

and safe among
warm meals broadloom a good school and
small crisp dresses

a better
new grown-up with her,
matinees and restaurant tables
still for three

and for crossing streets
hands holding on
both sides

surely happy often

at most sometimes
indirectly watchful
of friends' unvarying homes

or still, aloof a minute
from little-kid storyhours
that mention permanence

but not by any stretch
of the emotions
to be characterized by
a word like grief

and for sure not thinking, right now, about
the fleet of plasticine Chinese junks
sailing
across the floor of this upstairs cottage bedroom
I guess since the end of last summer

How We All Swiftly

My God how we all swiftly, swiftly
unwrap our lives, running from
one rummaged secret to the next
like children among their birthday stuff –
a shout, a half-heard gasp here
and for a while bliss somewhere else
when the one thing we asked for all year
is really there and practically as perfect
as we knew it would be. Those beckoning passes
into what's ahead: first words, the run
without a fall, a bike, those books,
a girl whose nakedness is endless in our bed,
and a few public stunts with results that
partly please us. And on we go, my God how
restlessly among glimpsed profiles turning and
undarkening towards us as we reach them – praiseworthy
the ones who'll press on with this, press on
so long and so often wrong, hoping to prove
some of the children right.

Death of Women

Everywhere they were just
wiped out. Supermarkets
hauled them away in shopping carts,
libraries and kindergartens closed
with unreassuring bulletins,
for as long as it lasted
husbands, waking, found them staring
at ceilings or sprawled in doorways
to the children's room, as if
it was there they had felt they must
explain hardest. Anthropologists
and all-night launderette manageresses,
a naked blackhaired princess
in a rocksinger's *Mitteleuropa* hunting lodge,
their faces unpredictably hinting
astonishing peace or war
in appointments of love and birth
and the gestures of the day –
they all went.
By the third day it was over.
Statistics were assembled, it was agreed
the world was altered.
Life began on the adjusted basis.

Then new women appeared.

Sampling from a Dialogue

Stopping by the bedroom wall he says God
damn it Marge (if that's her name), we have been through
this forty thousand times now let's have a new
line, I need to hear something different, and this odd
and, well, obviously it's inflated, analogy comes into his mind
– Roland, at Roncesvalles, and *his* last long call –
and he stands where he happens to be, beside the wall
and waits, he knows now he's listening for some kind
of miracle, what she's going to say,
one of them always finds a consoling pose
and his feel all used up, and he tries to picture those
horsemen, bright lances, rescuing armies on the way,
and from the bed behind him she says *Well*
maybe there is just such a thing as
having enough of somebody,
breaking the rhyme,
and both of them stay where they are, too far
apart again, in a clarity neither of them expected or
thought they were making, and listen to
the catastrophe of time.

William, etc.

William, Percy, Fred, George, Pawcel and Jack,
all brothers and all relatives of mine,
all bearing the Coles name and all lost at sea
on the same ship, same day, in the '14–'18 War,
too drenched for graves so six names on a plaque
in a rural Somerset church, the usual
one-line *Überschrift*, stonecutter's irony,
'Their Name Liveth For Evermore' –
would have been my uncles, once or twice removed,
if that day hadn't removed them before.

Think of all the cousins I might have had, and places
to be the caller-from-abroad in; or unfamiliar
anniversaries that girls who, old or dead now, may
have had to learn, and children's shapes and faces
hardly at all the same. Cancelled names on country
mailboxes, too, absences everywhere, you could say –
except for Davy Jones and those old watery arrangements,
what a jostling under 'C' that day!

Codger

Think what we like of him, dim old dawdler,
Main Street gazer, birdy shuffler –
stiff-collared, shiny-shoed – or say it,
his peace won't budge. He'll summon our dead betters
in dozens to smile us down, they know if we don't
who was there in livelier times and did his share,
helped give a shape to shouts all quiet now,
and what's more they won't change their minds.
That time the railroad almost picked another town,
meetings all night that week, and if you were there
you heard a few words from him, you bet you did;
two wars, one that he went to; and everybody's climb,
not easy, after the market bust in '29. And in a pinch,
what about Jack Thwaite, the curling rink that night,
and what *he* said? Spare with his praise, Jack Thwaite,
so everybody harked. They don't come any fairer
than Jack, and not just saying this on account of
those fine sentiments of his that night, either.
Felt that way about him for years.
                                    And one or two
girls, never mind them, when he was a stripling,
before Clara. But he remembers a woman
getting out of a car in winter, must be fifty years ago,
wore a little fur coat and looked him
straight in the eye when he came up.
He kept right on going, of course, but
boy, was *that* a look!

Not Just Words but World

Not just words but world grows simpler
as she dies. Now so much that
subtly loured or beckoned, the nightmare's
endless stumble or the threaded maze to favour,
obliterated. Gone the mornings and thousands
of afternoons, puzzle of years, patternless
after all. Now it's just a straight dash
for the dark, so late the wasteful agendas
of expectation laid by.

Only the small ones, perpetual, remain. Now
she's sure she should have sat, chin in her hand,
watching her son's new eyes move, the sunlight
on the floor; with untrammelled mind
more amply entered the early words; heedful
the smile for every homecoming. Does it matter?
Yes. Her daughter on the favourite roan pony,
cantering past, straightbacked and intent –
for that one, never such rapture since. Nothing
even close. Leave him, she should have told her,
all the bleak years. Of course she should,
and was so near to it so often. But
were all those nights like this one,
through her bedroom window slow fields of stars?
Those too. Those too.

Gull Lake, Alta.

'You just go out the door'
she said, 'and it's down there to the right.
Not a lake at all,
just a pond, really, but
lovely after supper.
Uncle Bert would walk down
with white towels when it was
dark. *Once more across and back,*
we'd call. He'd wave, and leave
the towels on the bank.'

                    Her old body
couldn't manage a dozen strokes now, and she's
three provinces away.

Those white towels on the bank!

The Prinzhorn Collection

Verwaltungsdirektor
Alte Staatsgalerie
München, 18 Januar, 1981

… Finally, let me kindle your
curiosity a little (may one say
'kindle'? I am grateful for any
corrections!) concerning our current
exhibition here. After *Der Blaue
Reiter,* so great a draw in the fall,
we have now – drawings, letters and
journals by the inmates of a nineteenth-century
Irrenanstalt (madhouse)! A worthy
doctor named Prinzhorn salvaged these
during his own tour of duty there
from the disregarded files of
a predecessor. *Mein Lieber,*
they are strong stuff.

The women's drawings, *zum Beispiel.**
You would suppose it an assigned
school exercise, so alike, soon so
almost-routine, are these fantasies!
The women picture themselves always
naked; very often kneeling; and time
after time their faces, averted from us
and curtained by manes of long, long
hair hanging down their backs – can it be
that it was never cut? – are pressed into
the unbuttoned flies of a plump,
moustached and be-medalled policeman.
The shaft of whose erection is occasionally
visible, in part of course. And who stands
impassive, stolid, unstartled. He expects
this. It is either his duty, or his right.

---

* for example

One thinks of Edvard Munch's women,
so often seen from the rear, their
backs a gleaming whiteness down which
a dark river of hair, a wide, slow
curve of it, moves; their mouths
similarly glued. Of course Munch
was called mad too. I have always
felt I knew what to think about that.
In truth, I believe I still do. But –
it is another layer, this, now,
is it not? I can hear you saying so!

Over the men's drawings here I draw,
not without predictable awkwardnesses,
a veil. As for the journals, the letters:
they record termless time. Complaints,
threats, fawnings, explanations, excuses,
prayers. Rational and irrational proposals.
Traüme und Alptraüme, dreams and
nightmares; the latter, literally translated,
'mountain-dreams' – a more powerful image
there, would you agree? No? 'Ah, these
Germans,' you murmur instead, 'how
they love powerful images!' Let us pass
uneasily on. In short, an entire human condition
is here, everything except utter despair.
Verzweiflung schreibt nicht, we say –
despair doesn't write. But from the borders
of despair, yes. Often, it seems. It is
the address from which many of these
dispatches are mailed. *To* nowhere. Only
to the Herr Direktor's pedantically indexed,
whisper-free files.

… Nowhere until now. And what strikes one

now, browsing through these derelict
hundred-year-old signals (airless cries, unlit
gestures) and with the bureaucratic moiety
of the dialogue at last, blackest of ironies,
not getting through, is that these writings
have the uncontested rhythms of truth. As if
after so many years muzzled very far down
in the dark, they have become transparent
and are unable to hide anything. And gazing
right through these transparencies, one sees
oneself. Choking.

Joseph Grebing. I could choose others,
I shall name only him. A dozen letters, almost
all to his father. Also a stupendous, illuminated
scroll, like a page from a Book of Hours, but
this one single-track, single-authored,
self-memorializing, and this self running nose-down
for redemption, breathing audibly, even panting;
the scroll hand-drawn and coloured in reds and blues,
more accurately in crimsons, lapis lazulis, indigoes;
listing Joseph G.'s academic honours, which although
modest are set down with *élan*, with *punctilio*;
and his unsullied *Herkunft* (pedigree, provenance);
and his outraged innocence. Yes, 'outraged' – this
document, at first glance merely a more vivid replica
of those ornate confections to be seen on the walls
of rustic solicitors, all penmanship and pomp and
the signatures of hapless mini-dignitaries, on closer
inspection reveals a smuggled subtext. A thin,
leaf-coloured tendril winds from one beflowered
upper-case letter to the next, and contains, like
an icon'd saint's girdle, messages – to speak plainly,
just one message, of unmistakable awfulness.
A message four words long, the four words repeated
over and over along that tendril's curlicued length,

ending where they begin and beginning again
where they end, and so elegant and near-runic in
design as to mislead the eye into believing them
there for the design's sole sake. This at-length
deciphered rune reads: *Du hast keine Idee Du hast
keine Idee Du hast keine Idee.*

Du hast keine Idee.

You have no idea.

The cunning of the workmanship, which
at first disguises, when found out enhances
the hysteria.

But I anticipate. It is not until his eighth
institutionalized year that this scroll engrosses
Joseph. Meantime, the letters.

*'Geehrter Vater,
Ich weiss nicht, ob du vergessen hast,
dass du einen Sohn hattest ...'*
– this is written six months after
his arrival. He is thirty-one years old. He will
continue writing letters until he is forty-three,
after which we know nothing more. He
stops. Simple. Chaos drinks him.
Drawings accompany many letters,
they continue until the forged opus
described above (his Chartres, his
angelic host, his thousand-mouth'd
Cry of the Innocents), then cease. What

---

* Honoured Father,
  I don't know if you have forgotten
  that you had a son ...

do the drawings show? Himself in
pastoral attitudes. A repetitive but not
disagreeable series. He is usually wearing
a lemon-coloured short-sleeved shirt, and
gazes directly out at us. Among haystacks.
By a stream. Tending sheep. Look,
he seems to say – while you watch, while
you walk by, I am here. While you
accomplish the seasons of your life. And yet,
und doch, the ubiquitous small figure appears
to be assuring us, See, I am good. I am small
under the blue sky. In my lemon-coloured
shirt, I am no trouble.

What do you think,
Lieber Freund, what is your professional
judgment? Do you suppose this is so?
Does the colour of his short-sleeved shirt
tell you this is how he is? Or do you suppose
this is not he at all, in this yellow shirt, turning
his button eyes towards us beside the unmolested
stream – ?

Perhaps they thought, the doctors,
the rapt curators of so much *entartete Kunst*,*
that it is a trick. An eight-year hoax! In this
yellow shirt there is nothing more than
a harmless *Doppelgänger*, set going by
a madman's brush. While the madman himself
watches touchily, wrathfully, from the shelter of
a neutral tint.

---

* A phrase coined by the Nazis to characterize art unacceptable
to the regime ('artless' or 'malformed' art, approximately); thus, most
non-representational art, Picasso, Max Ernst, and certainly most of the
'mad' drawings in the Prinzhorn collection.

'Father: This is the second year I write
to you at this season – '

'Father: Although I confess I was ill at ease
during all that month and thus disturbed
my fellow-workers, your employees,
for which I again apologize, still I did not
deserve this. It is too much. The noise
at night here, you have no idea. The *Gestank*.
The people.'

Or to his brother Paul. No one had visited him
that year, either. Or, for all he knew, or we know,
written.
'*Lieber* Paul: There is no good ground, merely
because I am taking no part in the business,
to ignore me. How willingly would I set forth
in the mornings beside you – '

Here is the last letter, written when he is forty-three.
'For the twelfth year I write at Christmastime.
I hope and pray you are well, also my mother.
I enclose a drawing of the scene I can so well
imagine – '

This crayoned drawing survives. One sees
that it was folded four-square, then once more,
to fit an envelope. A well-dressed man
sits in his parlour, hands clasped upon the head
of a walking-stick, seeming to approve as
a woman and several daughters decorate
a tree. One of the girls is standing, in
a long skirt, on a stepladder. Both her arms
reach up towards the top of the tree, where
she is fastening a star.

Finis Joseph Grebing, at least my account
of him. His testament – the above-listed
artefacts – was, as I have said, found in
the Herr Direktor's *Büro*. Nothing of it
was ever mailed, or we should not now
have it. The drawings. The letters. An
illustrated calendar, of which I may say
more when we meet. The self-portrait,
or, as it may be, the *Doppelgänger*,
he of the lemon-coloured shirt.
The certificate, icon, scroll, with
the leafy tendrils. *You have no idea.*
Along with the memorabilia of other
long-stay guests or personnel,
cf. that odd business of the guard,
as he undoubtedly was: moustache,
shaft, shiny medals, paunch.

A final ironic touch. The admirable
and eponymous doctor, Prinzhorn, has,
in a brief catalogue entry, the following
dates attached to his name: 1887–1933.
He seems to have been a humane man,
or he would not have been so struck (so
'stricken', I am almost sure I should say)
by his discoveries among his predecessor's
files, and we at the Galerie would have had to
seek out other images to hang on our walls
this New-Year season. This humaneness
admitted, one is bound to feel Doktor
Prinzhorn timed his death wisely. To have
soldiered on even a few years longer
would have meant risking learning worse news
still, and hearing an even more massive cry.

One would not wish him that, God knows.
Indeed, on either humanitarian or divine grounds
one would not wish God that. Though presumably
He already has it, has learned all and heard all,
never mind what one may wish.

Enough. *Basta*, the amateur metaphysics.
Not for me to meddle with. I return, stooping
a little, towards my competency, the visible.
The Prinzhorn Collection moves to Düsseldorf
in March, there are no plans for it after that,
it will be dismantled. A sculpture exhibition
is due here from Berlin at that time –
two young artists, a married couple in fact.
I know little of them. Perhaps you will come,
your students will be nice, they will allow you.
We will talk. Yes? Try. This long letter,
sorry. More *sang-froid* next time. I am
sorry for this.

Mishenka (in two versions) *

I   At sixteen, Niki, Leo's father-to-be, got,
from his parents, a Play-'n'-Learn
present: that is, a servant girl, who taught
him the necessary, and in return
became pregnant. This meant Niki was all right.
At least at night.

The baby, however, Mishenka, who, as fate
had it, lived, and grew up to become a kind
of stable boy, later coachman, on the family estate,
left, strange to say, not a rack behind –
strange, I mean, when you compare
the marvels his half-brother left. Although their

lives *did* diverge. This older one, who, as somebody said,
had a 'brutish' face, couldn't ever even have read
W & P, being illiterate, and he died
a pauper, two good reasons so far to decide
not to leave any messages – so if he forgave
the family, if he felt, ever, it had been more worry at how he'd behave

than real honest-to-God hardness of heart or unconcern,
well, we can't tell. The fact is, from such
as Nicholas Tolstoy's oldest son, we will learn
nothing of any of this. Or not much.
Something about sadness. Something that sinks
the heart a bit, is all. The rest's gone missing.
There's not a photo, or parting word, nothing to show what he thinks
about his child, if he ever had one. Nobody reminiscing.

---

* from 'Tolstoy Poems'

II At sixteen, Leo's father got
    a present from his parents.
    Sort of Play-'n'-Learn.
    This worked out pretty well.
    Meanwhile the present,
    a servant girl, duly became
    pregnant, had Mishenka.

    Mishenka, although older than Leo
    and, of course, his half-brother,
    never exactly became Leo's
    alter ego,
    no,
    he hung around the stables mostly,
    did not learn how to read or write,
    became a groom when he was old enough,
    developed a 'brutish' face,
    and to cap it all off
    died a pauper. How's that for
    dissimilar brothers?

Major Hoople

A grotesque, I knew.

Vainglorious and logorrhoeac, gassing away
from above his ballooning waistcoat
to lodgers sitting or standing in
attitudes of decorum-annulling scepticism.

He seemed to have no teeth; neither did
Martha, dirigible-wife. Their identical faces
were puddings. Hers was sensible and without
illusions. Two or three times a year she would
almost smile.

His harrumphing and egadding.
His fez. His spats.

The skinny boarders, travelling salesmen
by the unpremeditated look of them.
Proofs of their lostness were the lengthening
cigarette ashes, wilting towards
rumpled shirts. They had nobody
to warn them.

To what did I compare him? To
a home-derived image of man as
unmockable, the high seriousness
of middle years. By which standards
he would not do. So gross, so
little respected. He verged on
the repellent. He was barely human.
He was appalling.

But now he fills me with longing
for a safe and reliable time where
he meant all those things – and
age and failure too, star-distant then
from me as those – instead of
a caricatured but incontestable man.

And where beyond him, and beyond
the afternoon paper's large pages,
the smell of newsprint coming up close
as my arms spread wide to begin the last
orderly refolding, the lights have just come on
in the dining room. Soon a lost voice will say
come to supper.

Abandoned Lover

Whether he rushes vainly, or
crawls to weep, she is there.
In his belly or ribs she may
any minute begin again that walk
towards him, wearing that dress.
Her voice knows a hundred ways
to start. Along his forearms, perhaps,
her naked body surges in their
last lovemaking. Probably
this is worst. No, worst
is remembering she is somewhere,
doing new things.

Abrupt Daylight Sadness

Abrupt daylight sadness of one to whom
a small child says,'I love you
more than anybody else in the world.'
This is a father or a mother, usually –
at once they know there is nothing more to want here
forever, he knows this, she knows this,
they fly a short way towards real Heaven
but soon knowing it is more than they may
have or should desire, pause and fall
back. Sharp arrows from one too young
to know Time, the enemy.

Landslides (six excerpts)

Visits to the Gericare Centre

I As you steadily – startled
into reverie only when
the spoon nearly misses
your mouth – munch your way
through supper,

strapped up straight and fed
from a mashed bowl,
your eyes concentrating
as if to force
a devoted, furious someone

to appear,
far-travelled ransomer
with whom you soon must also be
far and travelling
(not as I am,

shuttered with memory and
with repeated enterings of this
room, also with thinking
of how the staircase
to the parking lot will look,

of an impending book or recent
sex – and you *convenable*, soon,
in after-hours stasis,
unable to turn over but staring out
over rubbishing years) –

who, when you go, will
guard that whole winter I
never left my bedroom or
the snow my window-ledge, kept
home from school

an endless, unachieving winter
to begin again, out of
childish muse and dream,
this old, hard business of
meddling with time?

IV There was a day when the leaves
were yellow under the rain,
not the very last leaves
but almost, you said what is
to be done

with this body, these legs that
trudge it here and there
to no purpose, when I compare,
you said, these purposes
with others, O

tiny and shameful,
it was a day when
many of the leaves were
a flat, soaked yellow
on the glistening black pavement

and you could still explain
what was going on, what was
happening, you could demonstrate
the wonders of a normal competence,
mine, say,

by your own slow-motion,
inexorable, sometimes even
comical
declension from it.
The driveway was

yellow with soaked leaves
and if you had ceased then
I would not be beginning, sitting
so near you here, to understand
the intimate cynicism of the world.

V Your face is between two mysteries.
   How death will be, your face
   in sprinting patches rusts
   towards it, it is wearing out
   towards one mystery.

   The other is just before
   I was born, I have studied
   the inaccessible sunlight
   on the veranda when I was almost
   there, your face watches

   my sister who is three years old and
   stands mildly within the sunlight,
   its prodigious composure
   has always eluded me.
   This is the other mystery.

III How human beings are alike
    in undefended states!
    No knowing how much you're
    hearing or understanding, but
    for an hour now

I have held your hand
and talked to you
of extreme things
– with silences between –
as you, in hours too early

in my life for me to give
accounting for, surely
with some comparable (privately
soaring) voice lulled or dreamed
me. As though we had,

those many years before,
leaned out to look and found
both of us (until both
faded there) listening from some
stupendous, covenanted place

to sounds too deep
for remedy. Those sounds are
burrowing but still audible,
it needs us both to
let them go.

X   There are no native speakers
    of this dialect. But I allow your
    mangled syllables to float towards
    words inside me,
    the slightest sound can do it.

    What I'm afraid of learning here is
    that the last images to fade show
    accumulated private damage. If you
    nod, if you even seem to agree,
    I will absorb it as truth.

Words like 'worth', 'dignity', etc.,
circle this ward like planets.
If these words are not dead, if
those planets are reachable, they are for
moated and convoyed travellers.

Over the car radio, report of
a white bear sighted forty miles off
Baffin, swimming away from land.
Tonight, driving towards you,
away from land.

XI When a breath of early freshness
    blows over you, even now
    when a breath of a kind of
    fullness re-opens the hiding-place
    behind the leaves –

    when he parted them
    to find you hiding there,
    even now when your young father
    parts the leaves,
    always his face

    bending close towards
    thrilled laughter –
    what kings, what legends!
    Who is here now to find you
    as you were,

    who is here to find you before
    the roamings into womanhood,
    to find you among the leaves?
    Press my hand if you know.
    Press it anyway.

Walking in the Snowy Night

You cannot imagine how I long for this creature. I dream of her every
night and wake with my heart all sore.
  – Thomas Mann, in a letter (about Katia, later his wife)

In this softfall of early night snow
this enveloping silence
this soundless drifting-down which continuously
obliterates even while I walk
the proof of my being here,

you cannot imagine how I
long for you.

Among all the exaggerations of art and snow
which veer past me down onto this
snow-narrowed sidewalk, seeming now
in this silence to curtain and shelter me
from my recent life

your imagined voice arrives saying
I love you. Saying *my love.*

I nearly fall down.

Obvious that these were the right sounds
even though they were only imagined –
the knee-deep white track I am following
which seemed about to rock up towards me
now steadies itself kindly.

So I listen again, here it comes, *I love you,*
this time a never-glimpsed panorama
of 'home' hollows me, the room of the world
down from which all these small irregular

fragments of white softness are drifting
rounds outwards with possibility.
There is nothing here except this undistracting
accumulation of white and these
simple thoughts of you
which I continue towards privately.

The streetlights have just come on.
What an unceasing veering down out of
the dim greyness up there above the lights!

I needed to renew myself like this with silence
and with thinking of you –
by now I have been in this whiteness so long
almost all the dark colours
have withdrawn from me.
How the old perplexing images have
dwindled off into the silence!
The whole shape of my face has changed,
now it understands only its preparation for you.

I must prevent your little subtle breasts from
being thought of
or all this may become less peaceful.

Somewhere Far from This Comfort

somewhere far from this comfort
ah, far from this,
myself, it is my long-ago self
far from here

such luck to be glimpsed there
I am in a field, a field
or it is instead my childhood
and not a field

but even to be glimpsed there
to be caught sight of at the last minute, perhaps,
before it is too dark
for a field, or for childhood

I turn my head, my head
and light moves over the field
I am like a lighthouse
turning my head

the light runs far off
swiftly over the fields
it lights up what was becoming all dark
lights the stretches of swift dark land

there I am there, right there
for a moment in the light
oh, I am sure it was I
as the light ran over me

what was I doing, doing
I seemed to be reading, or
talking, perhaps, talking
yes, words and light together

the words seemed like fields,
fields, but the dark entered them
almost at once, those words,
they filled up with darkness instead

it had hardly left them, the dark
and there it came again
so they had practically no chance
only for a moment in the light there they were

and now I am gone, or
preoccupied, yes, preoccupied
the light passed beyond me
while I was preoccupied

it ran ahead over the fields
they are empty of me now, they are only fields
though the light ran over them
anxious and swift as childhood

My Son at the Seashore, Age Two

He laughs and a breeze
lifts his hair. His face tilts up
towards what has happened
to his hair, that it should lift,
and his laugh goes. Why
is this happening, his suddenly
serious face wants to know, and
what is happening. But
all it is is a little breeze
lifting his hair for a few seconds,
a little breeze passing by
on its way to oblivion –
as this day is on its way there too,
and as that day, twenty years ago,
was, too.

Someone has stayed in Stockholm

Someone has stayed in Stockholm ever since
I left. He sold the motorbike (I used to
find it sheltered under plastic after rain,
I never knew who put that there and never tried
to find out, why not, I wonder? – ah, I was
rushing away from my image-free life,
is why) and eventually got a serious job,
he may even have married about when I did,
perhaps he married Caisa –
why not, why *wouldn't* he like
milky-skinned girls with red hair, was he
crazy or something? Now his Swedish is
perfect, his kids have both had their
stipendium-years in Paris, and he spends
summers on the west coast, at Tylösand,
near Bostad, they like it for its beach and
the big-time tennis every July. If he regrets
anything it's having failed to show up
back home for those two major deaths,
nothing to do with staving them off but
there's always that gap because
you didn't speak a remedying sentence
in time, right? And by now you've guessed
what it was. I could expand but I won't. Back
to him, some lunchtimes he walks along Strandvägen,
its elegant melancholy facades, he admires
the boats tied up there, if the sun's out there's
those tiny blindings off the water, and if
he wants to he can head for the Old Town and take
interesting ways back. But what else
has he done? Has he lain on his bed and
realized he has this whole unobserved life
to idle in? To turn his car
in directions I didn't, and bring
all those roads into the headlights?
What roads? That's the point! Fine, but

there are other things than motion,
you know. Yes but whatever his headlights
touch is a bonus, even that late-night fence-post
whitening and then lost again
shouldn't be underrated, every image makes
a special offer when it knows
you decided against it the first time. He
could simply be remembering an old half-hour
when he was bored in the schoolroom and
had a mysterious unfinished thought about
how his life will turn out – there's
nothing remarkable about this except that perhaps
he remembers it often whereas I'm only
remembering it now and only because of
him, because of the extra time he has. Or
he could be standing on the escalator and there's
a woman going the opposite way who
looks at him so intensely for
as long as it takes her to ride past
that he longs for her all day, or even
switches directions and catches up to her,
but what happens then? Who knows. Maybe
she says Oh that was just the look
I give men whose devotion I want for only
a few seconds, time's up, on the other hand
she could have recognized him from
some other life or escalator. But
this is what I mean. Whatever he does
is innocent because back there where he lives
he never waves or makes a sudden move, and this is
something I think about a lot and which
words cannot soothe. Although you can
fall into places deeper than language,
can't you? Yes. He has.

Forests of the Medieval World

Forests of the medieval world, that's
where her mind will wander
the three dissertation years, lucky girl –
Forest of Bleu, which crowded around
the walls of Paris and stretched 10,000 leagues
in every direction; the great Hercynian forests
of East Prussia, from which each year
334 drovers bore the logs for the fires
in the Grand Duke's castles of Rostock,
of Danzig and, furthest east of all, guarding
the borders towards the Polish marshes,
Greifswald and Wolgast. I'm so sad
I could die, you said as you left, but
my children, how could I bear it –
and I know, I know there are ways
of losing children, of seeing them stray off
among the trees even now, especially now!
Every fleet needed for its construction
the razing of an entire forest –
lost forests meeting on the tilting hills
of the Caspian, the Baltic, the Black Sea,
over the mountains of water the file of forests
comes. Your face is a mobile mischief,
do you know? Your eyes mocked before
they entreated, your lips rendered
both comedy and its dark twin
in microseconds, and your tongue
harried my mouth's bays and inlets.
The *Oberforstmeister* of Kurland promised
the King 'at least half-fabulous' beasts
for the hunt, his forest measured
140,000 *arpents* and even on the swiftest mounts
horsemen could not traverse it
in a month. My mind runs fast
down its *arpents* and leafy corridors,

seeing no one, I should slash
tree-trunks to procure my safe return
but I can't stop. My mind is running
on pure grief and pure love, I want you
to know this. The Forest of Othe
was so still you could hear a shadow
cross a face at sixty leagues' distance –
it had linked the Lyons Massif with
the Woods of Gisors but after a hurricane
levelled a million trees in 1519 the diligent
peasants moved in with plows and those forests
were never reunited. And
the forests of Finland, have you thought of those?
All the way to Archangel and the White Sea?
They can show you how you were
before these excuses. What can you do
about this, your exigent look said
in the doorway, I am going do you realize
I am going? And that both of us will survive this?
When the Swedes needed cash they cut down
the forests of Pomerania, the result in
many cases is sand-dunes. This for day-trippers
is nice, in your rented *Strandkorb* there is room
for everybody, also for dressing and undressing
when the beach is crowded. In the forest of Morois
Tristan lies with Iseult, they are waiting
for the King her husband who will tell history
they were only sleeping. In
the Black Forest dwarf trees and greenheart
still flourish – as for the Rominter Heide
it was so huge that most of its lakes
and forests were 'held in reserve',
not listed or even mentioned, so for generations
all that those lakes and forests could do was
grow uncontrollably in the imagination. I

would take you with me into the Rominter Heide
if you would come: there
each child we must not hurt will
wear a rose in sign of her ardent, forbearing
heart, in sign of his calm-eyed ascent through
our extreme, necessary years.

My Death as the Wren Library

I dreamt last night of my own
Death. As I died, I became the
Wren Library in Nevile's Court in
Trinity College, Cambridge. Dying,
The library became even more
Luminous, its splendid thinly leaded
Clerestory windows were lighting up
Even more valuably.

I tried to phone a cab
To go downtown but the line went
Dead!

My wife was moved. She had
A new friend already, however.

Sophie S., a friend of mine,
Though not that sort of friend,
Was even more moved. She found
A poem of mine describing all this
And rewrote it, in rhyming verse.
'Oh my little bicycle' was one of
Her lines. I knew I would not have
Published the poem in this form.

At a certain point I wept.
Up to this point I had kept my death
From everyone (although they knew).

When I wept the Wren Library
Did not tremble – I had feared
It would. Its clerestory luminosity,
Which was of course *my* clerestory
Luminosity, grew even more coolly
Elegant and uninhabited.

Its lack of inhabitants
Was what made its unearthly beauty
Glow so.

After my weeping, my wife and
Her new friend were more moved
Even than before.

        It was my heart,
The cause.

My son was in the general area.
In general, there was a feeling of
A certain amount of sorrow.

But I didn't want to worry
My son, who is fond of me,
And is eleven.

I was concerned about the taxi.
Would my beautiful windows oscillate
Too much on the trip downtown,
And shiver into thousands of
Tiny spears?

People were walking up and down
On the gravelled paths of
Trinity's Nevile's Court.

My death had been inevitable.

My son's face kept turning up,
Like a moon among all these things.

Self-Portrait at 3:15 a.m.*

A skinny old party in a too-big suit
has just turned the lights on
at a quarter past three. What
does he do now? Where is everybody?
He is just realizing nobody has told him
how to be as old as this. Another way
of putting it: nobody has taught old age
how to enter him. He's wondering
why has he painted himself into this room
which so obviously has got only
a few minutes left in it. Just inches
below the paint's surface in that canvas
over there the shadowy damp breasts
of that woman remind him of something.
Was it worth her while, once, to love him?
He remembers a night-fulcrum –
those breasts swaying close over his eyes
again and again, half the night it seems,
coming over like moons, his mouth too
was continuously amazed. He always knew
descriptions of happiness must remain illegible
but you can stay close to it if you don't move,
can't you? No you can't. These did, though –
glistening from his own young mouth, too;
an hour's immortal even if a life isn't.

---

* from 'The Edvard Munch Poems'
   (based on a painting of the same title by Edvard Munch)

Untitled

I awoke with a feeling of clarity, a feeling diaphanous as a lake at dawn, as clichéd as that but undismissable, the lake itself then spreading out before me. The sudden patience of it among that congestion of trees and low bushes – you knew your life should always have been like this.

From the opposite shore came sounds of several brief unapprehended lives.

The ten fingers of someone's two hands were pressing into my back like little warm pools.

Parts of many ideas were beginning to be visible to me.

I had not sustained any damage at all yet. Whatever was special in me had not been dulled by use or exposure or by being thought about. This was the main thing.

Nothing used to be better than it was now.

A vagueness on the shore of the lake was revealed as the sum of all happiness. Within a minute or two I knew this couldn't be true. But most happiness.

I was waiting for the images to start. There were no books, nobody had ever died, the first wave would soon think itself in from the lake.

Kingdom

for Luke

Around six, six-thirty these late winter days
I'm usually walking home across Lawrence fields,
couple of blocks from here. Make a point
of checking on the rink, the afternoon hockey guys
finished now and the last light fading off it,
though you can easily spot the gone-silent
sprayed brakings and prodigal wheelings incised
on the glow. I like it best when the Zamboni's
out there doing its ignored choreography,
blue lights glittering and the kid's dark head
turning to neither one side nor the other, just
intent on getting it right. Around one end and
up the middle and peel off, down the side
and up the pure broadening middle again,
lights glittering, kid's silhouette watching ahead.
He must like this. Nobody else around,
no older guy to shout advice or start anything.
A one-handed spin on the wheel takes him down
the far side. All along the streets the skaters
are at supper, they've abandoned their small
criss-crossing calls, terse celebrations, all
those rasping swiftnesses in exchange for their
ampler lives, and what's left is this,
slow dance of blue light in a darkening
space. He's going around the last bend
now. I head off. The perfect thing's
just about ready again.

Marie Kemp

In my dream I found Marie Kemp, her old-fashioned
ringlets and timeless big blue eyes, watching me
across the grade ten desks as she every so often, I
half believed then and choose now to fully believe,
did. The dream showed ringlets and eyes because
back then I had only a glimmering of more sequestered
things, but I remember her on tiptoes trying to reach
the top of the blackboard, such legs and everybody
intent, and somebody's loud whisper, 'I'd like to
introduce her to *my* brute' – and I can plain as day
still hear my fierce whisper back, 'X' (I haven't forgotten
his name, but this is no place to mention it), 'you are
the world's most gruesome slob.' I despised him a lot,
envied him a little – for his thoughts, in both cases.
No way did that introduction ever take place. Next
in my dream Marie was sitting on the ground and
my head was in her lap, and those legs, which obviously
I never touched, were folded beneath her. 'Marie, Marie,'
I said, and murmured my wish that we could have lain
like this long ago – she did not speak but appeared
composed. She came first in our class year after year
but left school for some stupid job before reaching
grade thirteen and I lost track of her, how could I have
allowed that to happen? In my dream I was inconsolable
that this had been so and wondered if we would have
come to grief had we behaved differently, had we
fallen in love, etc. – waking, it was the phrase
'come to grief' that I kept on thinking about. As if
you walk round a corner and there it is, you have
come to it, Grief. A bad sight.

      Perhaps I have avoided this, I told myself.
Though I was not sure.

Flowers in an Odd Time

Peasants, Gorky said, would pull up
a woman's skirts and tie them over her head,
leaving her naked from the waist down.
They called this 'turning her into a flower'.

Turgenev, a contemporary and of course
a countryman of Gorky's, would never have
recorded such a thing. He would have felt
this was beneath him.

But Gorky recorded it, and I, who admire
Turgenev a lot and Gorky not much, have now
recorded it too. I think this is because
some images flower for me even though
it would be better, on balance, if they did not.

Of course we live in an odd time. The *Guardian*
recently maintained that 'the weird and the stupid
and the coarse are becoming our cultural norm,
even our cultural ideal'.

As for Turgenev, he wrote, 'The honourable man
will finish by finding he has nowhere to live.'

Reading a Biography of Samuel Beckett

for Charles Israel

I'm lying here reading on my bed, which is
where I basically do all my reading,
privily stocking my mind with news from
Samuel Beckett's singular life, a life
that I'm now learning was also covertly
very kind; and every once in a while,
feeling half ironic and half puzzled, I let
the book fall to my chest and ask myself
why (apart from the unqualified joy I am
experiencing reading Samuel Beckett's
own words, much quoted here, which are
so manifestly more exact and in an odd way
nobler than the words I am normally
exposed to in any standing-up situation)
am I doing this? stocking my mind, I mean?
After all I am not young, gone are those
perpetual landscapes full of uncatalogued
wisdom-caches that would, for a long while
I took this for granted, sooner or later be
stumbled upon, nor is there anything
in my current circumstances that leads me
to suppose I will ever be able to hand on
to others, as a result of this reading,
possibly with some interesting additions,
a real sense of how it feels to be lying in
this cave of wonderfully nuanced language.
(Although 'You cannot feel better than this',
I could say. Or I could stick to saying, '*I*
could not feel better than this'. But nobody's
interested). *Take into the air my quiet breath*,
Keats wrote, and Samuel Beckett read that and
wanted to, and therefore did, write the same
words down again, so there are two men who
found those words and decided to write them
down, as if they answered something. And now
here is one more.

Nurseryschoolers

for Sarah

A familiar wending, rainbow of backpacks and anoraks
along a snowy path, and the usual trudging marshals
at the rear. Twitterings and sidesteps, small hops and
arm-linkings, and some of the faces lowered, diminutive
penitents. A couple of dozen micro-agendas are passing
below my window here, none of them too pressing
probably, all the good or bad moves that will some day
catch up with them are tiny at time's horizon still. A sign
lights up on the snow, INNOCENCE! it predictably blares,
the blue neon blinks knowingly upon my own palimpsested
twitterings, clatter of years, my own inrush of longing for
good moves, for bad moves, for small walks, arm-linkings,
for somebody at the back guaranteeing I'll be OK.
The children are almost all out of sight now, they're
inside the school or behind those clumps of bushes
near the door, heading towards their couple of dozen
identical afternoon assignments, and later it'll be
towards their near-identical walks or drives home,
and then for a decade, say, their still mostly shared
games, huddlings, small-group raptures, covenants –
only afterwards, afterwards,
after the casual last of all schooldays, after
the final trooping-out into that last afternoon's
jostle and sunlight, its insouciant goodbye cries,
then, ah then,
their endlessly diverging wanderings of the earth.

On a Caspar David Friedrich Painting
Entitled 'Two Men Observing the Moon'

They have been standing here, tiny hands
clasped behind tiny backs, gazing upwards
at a full moon ever since their arrival 179
years ago. My heart swells with – with what? –
envy, not much but some, also with admiration,
looking at them. So small and so undemanding –
this patch of stony ground has always contented them.
How full their heads are with moon-thoughts!
Though there is more to be said. I for instance
who all my life have been discarding
patches of ground, stony or picturesque makes
no difference, have of late begun gazing upwards
fairly often, more than I used to, I would say,
thinking harmless thoughts. If I had been glimpsed
even one of those times, just then, or then, or
that other time, by someone who walked on past
and never turned to look again,
I'd live in that one mind forever serene as these,
a thought I'll keep. I could say more
but they show me there's no need.
How the moon shines! How the two men observe!
And how willingly would I have spent my life
as they have, murmuring small comments
to my friend as the years pass!

Botanical Gardens

Here's a handy Arcadia, let's go in.
Rich loamy smell, heavy fronds –
I'll hold this one up while you bend
through. *Frangula siliquastrum* –
fissured trunk, glossy blunt leaves, and
what an odd angle to this low branch, jutting
forward like a warning arm. Abandon all hope,
short people. Loamy smell, damp clumps
of humus, encroaching blunt leaves – and this
Latinate taxonomy in old brown ink. No,
go on ahead – I'll loiter a bit. A deep
breath. Roots, darkness. Another. What
fills me? Unself fills me. Breathfuls of
dark oblate leaves, clotted humus, forests.
Of course, yes, *trackless* forests. These
are people-proscribing smells. Nothing
here doubts itself, from which it follows
there is not a hint of me here. And not
a hint – what relief! – of many things
I'm sick to death of, e.g., vanity, anxiety
concerning perhaps some unfavourable
thing that has been said about me, general
unsettledness … a dozen such abstractions.
Contemptuous, derisory of all these, of
comparisons, rankings, restiveness,
Frangula siliquastrum has been here
all morning, also yesterday, also last year.
Decades, probably. My whole life. Sudden
remorse now on my part at not having lived
patiently enough. Steadfastly enough. Here
is such constancy, such fidelity. Easy,
though, for *Frangula siliquastrum*.

Still, something's going on. I am aware of
a reproof. All this verges on the valuable
and I will go on thinking of it, and yet
what is the point? There is no dialogue
here. Trees exclude us totally – woods and forests
are obscure in their permissions. This
has gone far enough, I think. I never wanted
to stay long anywhere, really.

Editor's Notes

1. With a few exceptions, versions of poems in this selection are the ones last published: poems from *Forests of the Medieval World* and *Kurgan* are as they appeared in those collections, and poems from the first six books as they were revised in 2005 for *How We All Swiftly*. However 'Sampling from a Dialogue' appears in the *Kurgan* version, and further changes (mostly small, sometimes reinstating features of earlier versions) have been made to 'Photograph from a Stockholm Newspaper ...', 'How We All Swiftly', 'Codger', 'Not Just Words but World', 'The Prinzhorn Collection', 'Landslides' and 'Someone has stayed in Stockholm'.

2. In his early books, Don Coles followed the old style of capitalizing the beginning of each verse line, something he mostly abandoned in his later work and in the reissue of his first six collections in *How We All Swiftly*. The caps survive in a few poems in *Forests of the Medieval World*, including one in this selection ('My Death as the Wren Library') and Coles has chosen to keep them here. I agree that they add something indefinable to the character of this poem.

About Don Coles

Don Coles was born April 12, 1927,* in the town of Woodstock, Ontario, to Alice Brown and Jack Coles, the second of four children. (Another might-have-been brother, stillborn, preceded Coles by a year and is the subject of one of his poems.) His paternal grandfather came to Canada from England at the tender age of fifteen, worked in various cities to save money to start a business, and eventually settled in Woodstock, where he built up the E.J. Coles company, a large department store (later sold, under duress, to Eatons.) Both of Coles' parents attended university; his mother was top girl in her graduating year. His father was a fine athlete (Coles too played serious basketball and tennis, the latter from early childhood to this day.) His mother was the literary influence and had the library, which included Thomas Hardy, Willa Cather, Chekhov, Balzac – works Coles read his way through during his teens. The quality of education in Woodstock was, in his words, 'not remarkable.... My mother took the place of that marvellous English teacher I never had.'

Coles entered Victoria College at the University of Toronto in 1945, a year when returning veterans greatly outnumbered teenaged freshmen. He did a four-year history degree, then a two-year M.A. in English, spending two undergraduate summers in Trois-Pistoles, Quebec, learning French, and one summer travelling in Europe. He had several courses with Northrop Frye and Marshall McLuhan, whom he recalls as the best teachers of his life. In between the two M.A. years, he spent a year in London working in a bookstore, then enrolled at Cambridge from 1952 to 1954, and upon graduating was awarded a British Council grant to live in Florence for a year. When that ended, a chance trip to Stockholm led to a several-year sojourn in Scandinavia, where he worked mostly as a translator. It was in Stockholm that he met Heidi Gölnitz of Lübeck, Germany, whom he eventually married; they lived in Copenhagen and Switzerland before coming to Canada with their daughter in 1965 – supposedly for a visit, but they stayed. A son was born in Toronto.

---

* erroneously recorded as 1928 in other sources

By this time Coles had read prodigiously, learned several languages, and written three or four full-length plays 'of no interest to anyone' (plus a one-act verse play he still periodically rereads), as well as two unpublished novels. A chapter of one of the novels had appeared in *Tamarack Review*, however, and was the basis on which he was offered a teaching position in Humanities at Toronto's York University. He accepted with some ambivalence, found he liked teaching a great deal, and remained at York until his retirement in 1996, teaching European literature and later, creative writing, in the program he helped start and directed for six years. He also served as poetry editor for the Banff School of Fine Arts from 1984 to 1994.

It was only around 1967, in tandem with teaching, that Coles began writing poems. His first collection appeared in 1975 when he was forty-seven. It was followed quietly by several others, but he resisted becoming any kind of public poet-persona. He was sixty-five when *Forests of the Medieval World* won Canada's premier literary award. As a poet, Coles has always marched to his own drummer. In an era of canon-revision he was not shy about inviting 'dead white males' into his poems, where they are treated like living familiars. He did not jump on the bandwagon of Canadian nationalism. He was never enamoured of the modernist poets, looking instead to what he has termed the 'Hardy-Larkin line', those who were able to move their art back towards accessibility and the general reader. Besides his ten poetry collections, Coles has, since retirement, published a novel and a collection of essays and reviews, and translated a late collection by the Swedish poet Tomas Tranströmer, with whom he has maintained a long friendship.

Coles resides in Toronto, but has lived (counting sabbaticals spent mostly in Cambridge) close to twenty years in western Europe, with sojourns in Munich, Hamburg, and Zurich besides cities already mentioned. He now tries to spend a month each spring in London, 'doing galleries or simply well-remembered streets in the mornings, theatre matinees most afternoons, and dining off Marks & Sparks meals with a halfbottle of wine and a book or the tely in the evenings; bliss, really.' A deeply private man, he lists family first among his pleasures.

— R S

Don Coles: A Bibliography

POETRY

Sometimes All Over (1975)
Anniversaries (1979)
The Prinzhorn Collection (1982)
Landslides: Selected Poems 1975–1985 (1986)
K. in Love (1987)
Little Bird (1991)
Forests of the Medieval World (1993)
Someone Has Stayed in Stockholm: New and Selected Poems (U.K., 1994)
Kurgan (2000)
How We All Swiftly: The First Six Books (2005)

TRANSLATION

For the Living and the Dead (1996)
  Poems, from the Swedish of Tomas Tranströmer (bilingual edition)

FICTION (Novel)

Doctor Bloom's Story (2004)

ESSAYS

A Dropped Glove in Regent Street: An Autobiography by Other Means (2007)

IN TRANSLATION

Die Weissen Körper der Engel (Sweden, 2007)
  Selected Poems, German translation by Margitt Lehbert,
  with parallel English text